MW01233318

CHANGING SEASONS

To everything there is a season,
and a time to every purpose under
   the heaven:

A time to be born, and a time to die;
a time to plant, and a time to pluck up
   that which is planted.

A time to love, and a time to hate;
a time of war, and a time of peace.

He hath made every thing beautiful
in his time. . . .

From Ecclesiastes 3

ideals

Ideals Publishing Corp.
Nashville, Tennessee

CHANGING SEASONS

ACKNOWLEDGMENTS

THE BEAUTY OF NATURE by John Burroughs. Reproduced from Tamarack Press with permission from Wisconsin Tales & Trails, Inc., Madison, WI; SONG OF THE WHEAT from *BETWEEN ETERNITIES* by Grace Noll Crowell. Copyright 1944 by Harper & Row, Publishers, Inc.; THE WAKING YEAR by Emily Dickinson. Reprinted by permission of the publishers and the Trustees of Amherst College from *THE POEMS OF EMILY DICKINSON*, edited by Thomas H. Johnson, Cambridge, Mass.: The Belknap Press of Harvard University Press. Copyright 1951, © 1955, 1979, 1983 by the President and Fellows of Harvard College; AUTUMN FIELD by Viney Wilder Endicott. Published by Warp Publishing Co., Minden, NB. Used by permission of the author; BAREFOOT DAYS by Rachel Field. Copyright 1926 by Doubleday & Company from the book *TAXIS AND TOADSTOOLS*. Reprinted by permission of the publisher; HOLLY FAIRIES by Aileen Fisher. Reprinted from *CHRISTMAS PLAYS AND PROGRAMS*, copyright © 1960, 1970 by Aileen Fisher. Plays, Inc., Publishers, Boston, MA; THE ROAD NOT TAKEN by Robert Frost. Copyright 1916, © by Holt, Rinehart and Winston. Copyright 1944 by Robert Frost. Reprinted from *THE POETRY OF ROBERT FROST*, edited by Edward Connery Lathem, by permission of Henry Holt and Company, Inc.; HOW I LEARNED THE MEANING OF LOVE from *THE STORY OF MY LIFE* by Helen Keller, 1954. Ued by permission of Doubleday & Company, Inc.; HOW WONDERFUL ARE ISLANDS from *GIFT FROM THE SEA* by Anne Morrow Lindbergh. Copyright © 1955 Anne Morrow Lindbergh. Reprinted by permission of Pantheon Books, a Division of Random House, Inc.; A SEASON OF REFLECTION by John Muir from *THE MOUNTAINS OF CALIFORNIA* by John Muir, copyright 1911 by The Century Co., New York; BELIEF by Garnett Ann Schultz from her book *AND THEN THE DAWN*; BARE BOUGHS and NOVEMBER WOODS from *QUIET REFLECTIONS AND TRANQUIL MOMENTS*, copyright 1979 by Patience Strong, published by Ideals Publishing Corporation. Used by permission of Rupert Crew Limited, London, England; SEPTEMBER COMES IN QUIETLY by Gladys Taber. Copyright © 1962 by Family Circle, Inc. Reprinted by permission of Brandt & Brandt Literary Agents, Inc.; ICE by Edwin Way Teale, reprinted by permission of Dodd, Meade & Company, Inc., from *A WALK THROUGH THE YEAR*, copyright © 1978 by Edwin Way Teale. Our sincere thanks to the following whose addresses we were unable to locate: W. T. W. Barbe for MOUNTAIN PINES; Amanda Barrickman for TULIPS; Cecil Brown for THE OLD HOMETOWN; Ethel Beal Caulfield for WAYSIDE; Sam Churchill for WHAT IS SPRING?; Kunigrande Duncan for OCTOBER SONG; George Z. Keller for THE BROOK; Margaret Elizabeth Sangster for CHRYSANTHEMUMS; Martha D. Tourison for RETURN OF SPRING.

Special Offer

Ideals Publishing Corp. offers a clear acrylic reading stand for only $7.95 to protect and feature your copy of *Changing Seasons*. Order product #ID10716, make your check payable to Ideals Publishing Corp., and send the order information with your name and mailing address to:

Catalog Department
Ideals Publishing Corp.
P.O. Box 148000
Nashville, TN 37214-8000

ISBN 0-8249-1067-2
Copyright © MCMLXXXVII by Ideals Publishing Corp.
Nelson Place at Elm Hill Pike
Nashville, TN 37214
All rights reserved.
Printed and bound in U.S.A.

Cover Photo
MOODUS RESERVOIR
MOODUS, CT
Fred M. Dole Productions

CONTENTS

SPRING

SUMMER

AUTUMN

WINTER

IRON COUNTY, WI
Appel Color Photography

GREENFIELD HILL, CT
Fred M. Dole Productions

A season of awakening, a physical rebirth that allows nature to throw off the burden of winter and take that first, fresh breath of a new season.

Could We Forget?

Why is it every springtime seems so new?
We know the crocuses will bloom again
And buttercups beside the pasture fence
Will call to golden tulips in the lane,
And yet when spring comes creeping down the trees,
We are surprised and wonder still at these.

Do we forget, when winter days are long,
The marshy places where the lilies lie
Under the ground and quiet banks of snow,
Waiting for spring to call across the sky?
Do we forget, because the nights are long,
The thrilling wonder of a robin's song?

Oh, yes, as long as spring comes back to earth
We will rejoice at miracles like these,
That brown wet earth can yield a lily cup,
That birds will build their houses in the trees,
And every twig and bush and living thing
Will answer to the throbbing call of spring.

Edna Jaques

Photo Opposite
CROCUSES
FPG International

Miracle of Spring

If you listen, if you lean close
　　To the singing, springtime earth,
You can hear faint muffled voices,
　　You can hearken sounds of mirth;
For above the running water
　　Souls of grass and shrub and tree
Are now lifting through the darkness
　　In a mystic symphony.
In the shadows of the woodland,
　　In the valley, on the hill,
You can hear the green grass whisper
　　To the waking daffodil;
And anemones are leaning
　　To the songs the lilacs sing,
As the earth lifts from its sleeping
　　In the miracle of spring.

　　　　　　　　Edgar Daniel Kramer

COUNTRY PATH
Jack Zehrt

Return of Spring

The winds of March are melting streams
And whipping pools to froth with snow,
While waiting April sleeps and dreams.

On swaying branch the yellow gleams,
The willows are the first to know
The winds of March are melting streams.

At dawn the maple grove has teams
Of men to draw the sap's swift flow,
While waiting April sleeps and dreams.

The doves are cooing 'neath the beams,
And cattle soon to fields will go.
The winds of March are melting streams.

The bees are restless, for it seems
Their honey store is sadly low,
While waiting April sleeps and dreams.

From fog and mist arise the steams
That nurture stirring life below.
The winds of March are melting streams,
While waiting April sleeps and dreams.

Martha D. Tourison

Photo Overleaf
ANZA DESERT STATE PARK, CA
Josef Muench

Photo Opposite
NORTH POMFRET, VT
Fred Sieb Photography

Blossoms in Springtime

So barren and bleak through the winter,
The victims of freezing and storm;
Frail branches reach prayerfully upward
And wait for new buds to take form.

Each tenuous shoot pushes boldly,
Destroying the walls of its tomb;
New life shall explode from its prison
And suddenly burst into bloom.

The born-again blossoms in springtime—
Wild seeds sprouting up through the sod
Will display through magnificent beauty
The splendid creation of God.

Kay Long

Photo Overleaf
JASPER NATIONAL PARK
ALBERTA, CANADA
Bob Clemenz

Photo Opposite
CHERRY BLOSSOMS
BELLEVILLE, NJ
Gene Ahrens

Tulips

Cup-shapes of yellows and reds
Are springing from long-silent beds;
And bell-shapes of lavender hue
(Intending the spirit to woo)
Are opening slowly to view.

While nodding in fields of new grass,
And blooming in beauty to last
For only the briefest of hours,
Sweet tulips! Your rainbow of flowers
Has brightened this landscape of ours.

Amanda Barrickman

Photo Opposite
TULIPS
Bob Taylor

SPRING: *A Season of Promise*

TULIP FARM
MOUNT VERNON, WA
Ed Cooper Enterprises

A season of promise, of new sights and sensations, of new chances, of renewed happiness, and of life.

What Is Spring?

Spring is a precise and delicate thing.

It is the touch of pink in an apricot bloom; the golden smile of a daffodil; water in an irrigation canal; the sound of a tractor in a field.

It is the way you feel when you get up in the morning; the glint of sunlight on a windowsill; the underground noise robins hear as worms work their way below the surface of a lawn.

Spring is seed going into the ground; or laughter of children.

It is big, fluffy clouds coasting across the sky; raindrops making rings in a puddle.

Spring isn't something you check out on a calendar, or are alerted to by the *Farmer's Almanac.*

It's a gentle stirring, deep inside, that insists you walk instead of waiting for a bus.

It's that fleeting moment of time, each year, when you suddenly become you.

It's when you say "Good morning" and mean it.

It's a moment of goodwill and pleasant thoughts.

It's when God speaks and you can hear him.

Sam Churchill

Photo Opposite
AMERICAN PAINTED LADY BUTTERFLY
Gay Bumgarner

A Season of Promise

My Heart's in the Highlands

My heart's in the Highlands, my heart is not here;
My heart's in the Highlands a-chasing the deer;
A-chasing the wild deer, and following the roe,
My heart's in the Highlands, wherever I go.
Farewell to the Highlands, farewell to the North,
The birth place of Valour, the country of Worth,
Wherever I wander, wherever I rove,
The hills of the Highlands forever I love.

Farewell to the mountains high covered with snow;
Farewell to the straths and green valleys below;
Farewell to the forests and wild hanging woods;
Farewell to the torrents and loud pouring floods.
My heart's in the Highlands, my heart is not here,
My heart's in the Highlands a-chasing the deer;
Chasing the wild deer, and following the roe;
My heart's in the Highlands, wherever I go.

Robert Burns

YANKEE BAY BASIN
POTOSI MTS., CO
H. Armstrong Roberts, Inc.

The Waking Year

A Lady red—amid the Hill
Her annual secret keeps!
A Lady white, within the Field
In placid Lily sleeps!

The tidy Breezes, with their Brooms
Sweep vale—and hill—and tree!
Prithee, My pretty Housewives!
Who may expected be?

The Neighbors do not yet suspect!
The Woods exchange a smile!
Orchard, and Buttercup, and Bird—
In such a little while!

And yet, how still the Landscape stands!
How nonchalant the Hedge!
As if the "Resurrection"
Were nothing very strange!

Emily Dickinson

Photo Overleaf
STERLING FOREST GARDENS
TUXEDO, NY
Fred Sieb Photography

Photo Opposite
BLEEDING HEART
Peregrine Photo Art

I Wandered Lonely As a Cloud

I wandered lonely as a cloud
   That floats on high o'er vales and hills,
When all at once I saw a crowd,
   A host of golden daffodils
Beside the lake, beneath the trees,
Fluttering and dancing in the breeze.

Continuous as the stars that shine
   And twinkle on the Milky Way,
They stretched in never-ending line
   Along the margin of a bay:
Ten thousand saw I, at a glance,
Tossing their heads in sprightly dance.

The waves beside them danced, but they
   Outdid the sparkling waves in glee;
A poet could not but be gay
   In such a jocund company;
I gazed—and gazed—but little thought
What wealth the show to me had brought.

For oft, when on my couch I lie,
   In vacant or in pensive mood,
They flash upon that inward eye
   Which is the bliss of solitude;
And then my heart with pleasure fills,
And dances with the daffodils.

William Wordsworth

Photo Overleaf
MENDOCINO COAST, C
Ed Cooper Enterprises

Photo Opposite
DAFFODILS
SOUTHWESTERN PA
H. Armstrong Roberts, Inc

Daisies

Daisies have a special place
   Within the human heart,
And memory recalls the joy
   That daisies can impart.

Tiny girls painstakingly
   Braid daisies in their hair
Or weave them into chains which they
   Insist they have to wear.

How many little boys have picked
   A gold and white bouquet
Which loving mothers rearranged
   For prominent display?

The game of "love me, love me not"
   Is played with petals white,
But daisies never, never tell
   Which answer may be right.

Daisies have a heart of gold.
   I guess that must be why
They grow profusely everywhere
   In fields that meet the sky.

                    Dorothy Butler Kimball

Photo Overleaf
MAGNOLIA GARDEN
SOUTH CAROLINA
FPG International

Photo Opposite
DAISIES
CHERRYFIELD, ME
Robert Holland

The First Spring Morning

Look! Look! the spring is come:
Oh, feel the gentle air,
That wanders thro' the boughs to burst
The thick buds everywhere!
The birds are glad to see
The high unclouded sun:
Winter is fled away, they sing,
The gay time is begun.

Adown the meadows green
Let us go dance and play,
And look for violets in the lane,
And ramble far away
To gather primroses
That in the woodlands grow,
And hunt for oxlips, or if yet
The blades of bluebells show.

There the old woodman gruff
Hath half the coppice cut,
And weaves the hurdles all day long
Beside his willow hut.
We'll steal on him, and then
Startle him, all with glee
Singing our song of winter fled
And summer soon to be.

Robert Bridges

Photo Overleaf
MT. RAINIER, WA
Ed Cooper Enterprises

Photo Opposite
FORGET-ME-NOTS
MORRISTOWN, NJ
Gene Ahrens

Spring

How beautiful the greening hills
And pastures lying in between.
Wild flowers are blooming everywhere,
And trees put on new leaves of green.
Up over all this varied hue,
There is a canopy of blue.

Spring is a birth time for the world...
A resurrection of new hope,
Where beauty rhymes with changing growth
And seems to add a wider scope.
Then over all and reaching high,
There is a canopy of sky.

Agnes Davenport Bond

Photo Opposite
STODDARD, NH
Dick Smith

SUDBURY, VT
FPG International

A season of abundance, of growth and natural beauty which comes with the summer sun.

Artistry

Glad summertime is graced with artistry
Of flowers in multi-rhythmed tracery
Like fragile balls of white and purple phlox,
And blushing faces of tall hollyhocks;
Long spears of foxglove reaching high
And meadow daisies laughing at the sky;
Bright flares of asters, charming and sedate,
And shy petunias by the garden gate,
Red roses throwing perfume to the breeze
While honeysuckle caters to the bees.
The morning glories awaken with the sun
And four-o'clocks tell when the day is done.
These are the strokes of life and hope, the lines
Glad summertime artistically designs.

Harold A. Schulz

Photo Overleaf
BRYCE CANYON NATIONAL PARK, U
Grant Heilman Photography, Inc.

Photo Opposite
MIDSUMMER MAGIC
Bob Coyle

Nature's Beauty

The beauty of nature includes all that is called beautiful, as its flower; and all that is not called beautiful, as its stock and roots.

Indeed, when I go to the woods or the fields, or ascend to the hilltop, I do not seem to be gazing upon beauty at all, but to be breathing it like the air. I am not dazzled or astonished; I am in no hurry to look lest it be gone. I would not have the litter and debris removed, or the banks trimmed, or the ground painted. What I enjoy is commensurate with the earth and sky itself. It clings to the rocks and trees; it is kindred to the roughness and savagery; it rises from every tangle and chasm; it perches on the dry oak stubs with the hawks and buzzards; the crows shed it from their wings and weave it into their nests of coarse sticks; the fox barks it, the cattle low it, and every mountain path leads to its haunts. I am not a spectator of, but a participator in it. It is not an adornment; its roots strike to the center of the earth.

John Burroughs

Photo Overleaf
PACIFIC GROVE, CA
FPG International

Photo Opposite
LUPINES
MT. RAINIER NATIONAL PARK, WA
Gene Ahrens

Barefoot Days

In the morning, very early,
   That's the time I love to go
Barefoot where the fern grows curly
   And grass is cool between each toe,
      On a summer morning-O!
      On a summer morning!

That is when the birds go by
   Up the sunny slopes of air,
And each rose has a butterfly
   Or a golden bee to wear;
And I am glad in every toe —
      Such a summer morning-O!
      Such a summer morning!

Rachel Field

Photo Overleaf
QUEEN ELIZABETH PARK
VANCOUVER, BRITISH COLUMBIA
Ed Cooper Enterprises

Photo Opposite
SARA HARTSHORN ARBORETUM
SHORT HILLS, NJ
Gene Ahrens

Wayside

Some folks like city pavements,
  The hurrying to and fro,
But give to me the country lanes
  Where sweet wildflowers grow.

A winding pathway through the hills,
  A pool or sunny glen,
Where I may romp or dream awhile...
  And be a child again.

Where each hill is a mountain
  Touching the very sky,
And fleecy clouds, like magic ships,
  To fairyland sail by.

It's June, you know, so take my hand
  And we will wander far
Into the land of make-believe,
  Forgetting things that are.

Leaving the city pavements,
  The hurrying to and fro,
We'll find the country wayside
  Where sweet wildflowers grow.

Ethel Beal Caulfield

Photo Overleaf
LUPINES AND POPPIES
FPG International

Photo Opposite
COLUMBINE ON MAROON BELL MOUNTAIN
SNOWMASS WILDERNESS, CO.
H. Armstrong Roberts, Inc.

Yellow Is the Color of Summer

Yellow is the color of summer;
Surely it is so
When black-eyed susans and buttercups
As mini-suns brightly glow.

I see it in the hearts of daisies,
The skin of a ripening pear,
Corn on the cob at picnics,
Wisps of baby hair.

Yellow is happy and shining,
A carousel ride all the while.
Yellow, the color of summer,
I see in your sunny smile.

Violet Bigelow Rourke

Photo Overleaf
GARDEN DELIGHTS
Gay Bumgarner

Photo Opposite
PRICKLY PEAR CACTUS
Josef Muench

Song of the Wheat

The wind's deft fingers pluck the golden strings,
And music runs like light along the wheat:
Laughter is there and a bright gladness sings
An ancient song of fields that are replete
In their fulfillment where each golden head
Is rife with the precious essences of bread.

It is the song of wheat, a song of praise
For sun and moon and stars and clear cool rain,
For the heady ecstasy of summer days,
For long dark nights and perfect growing grain,
And for the earnest labor that distills
Those essences in far-off shining mills.

A song of future loaves, well-baked, to feed
A hungry world in its stark, desperate need.

Grace Noll Crowell

Photo Opposite
SNOHOMISH COUNTY, WA
Ed Cooper Enterprises

KAMIAK BUTTE COUNTY PARK, WA
Gene Ahrens

A season of affirmation, a time to
appreciate the splendor of God's gifts and
to accept the warmth of the season.

How Wonderful Are Islands

How wonderful are islands! Islands in space, like this one I have come to, ringed about by miles of water, linked by no bridges, no cables, no telephones. An island from the world and the world's life. Islands in time, like this short vacation of mine. The past and the future are cut off; only the present remains. Existence in the present gives island living an extreme vividness and purity. One lives like a child or a saint in the immediacy of here and now. Every day, every act, is an island, washed by time and space, and has an island's completion. People, too, become like islands in such an atmosphere, self-contained, whole and serene; respecting other people's solitude, not intruding on their shores, standing back in reverence before the miracle of another individual. "No man is an island," said John Donne. I feel we are all islands — in a common sea.

Anne Morrow Lindbergh

Photo Overleaf
STONE LAGOON
REDWOOD NATIONAL FOREST, CA
Ed Cooper Enterprises

Photo Opposite
CANNON BEACH, OR
H. Armstrong Roberts, Inc.

Summer

Winter is cold-hearted,
Spring is yea and nay,
Autumn is a weathercock
Blown every way.
Summer days for me
When every leaf is on its tree;

When Robin's not a beggar,
And Jenny Wren's a bride,
And larks hang singing, singing, singing
Over the wheat fields wide,
And anchored lilies ride,
And the pendulum spider
Swings from side to side;

And blue-black beetles transact business,
And gnats fly in a host,
And furry caterpillars hasten
That no time be lost,
And moths grow fat and thrive,
And ladybirds arrive.

Before green apples blush,
Before green nuts embrown,
Why one day in the country
Is worth a month in town;
Is worth a day and a year
Of the dusty, musty, lag-last fashion
That days drone elsewhere.

Christina Rossetti

Photo Overleaf
SEA STACKS
BANDON, OR
George Schwartz

Photo Opposite
IRIS
Fred Sieb Photography

Queen Anne's Lace

Lovely flower, to my ear,
Tell the secret I would hear!
What subtle fingers wove the thread
To make the lace around your head,
Then pinned upon your finery
That dazzling jewel, the bumblebee?
I have looked and found nowhere
A fabric fashioned with such care
And worn with such an airy style
The passing byways turn and smile.
If in such lace I could be seen,
I, like you, would look a queen!

Grace Tall

Photo Opposite
QUEEN ANNE'S LAC
H. Armstrong Robert

How I Learned the Meaning of Love

I remember the morning that I first asked the meaning of the word, "love".... I had found a few early violets in the garden and brought them to my teacher. Miss Sullivan put her arm gently around me and spelled into my hand, "I love Helen."

"What is love?" I asked.

I smelt the violets in her hand and asked, ... "Is love the sweetness of flowers?"

"No," said my teacher.

Again I thought. The warm sun was shining on us.

"Is this not love?" I asked.... It seemed to me that there could be nothing more beautiful than the sun.... But Miss Sullivan shook her head....

A day or two afterward I was stringing beads of different sizes in symmetrical groups. I had made many mistakes, and Miss Sullivan had pointed them out again and again with gentle patience...Miss Sullivan touched my forehead and spelled with decided emphasis, "Think."

In a flash I knew that the word was the name of the process that was going on in my head. This was my first conscious perception of an abstract idea.

For a long time I was still.... I was...trying to find a meaning for "love" in the light of this new idea. The sun had been under a cloud all day...but suddenly the sun broke forth in all its southern splendor.

Again I asked my teacher, "Is this not love?"

"Love is something like the clouds that were in the sky before the sun came out," she replied.... "You cannot touch the clouds, you know, but you feel the rain and know how glad the flowers and thirsty earth are to have it after a hot day. You cannot touch love either; but you feel the sweetness that it pours into everything...."

The beautiful truth burst open my mind. ... I felt that there were invisible lines stretched between my spirit and the spirits of others.

Helen Keller

Photo Opposite
PHLOX
FPG International

AUTUMN PREPARATION
NEW ENGLAND COUNTRYSID
FPG International

A *season of gathering, a time to collect nature's bountiful harvests and to admire the beauty of colorful falling leaves.*

A Time Called Autumn

Now, in the time of autumn,
When the harvest days are past,
When the scarlet leaf grows crisper
And the golden hours can't last,

There comes a time for sleeping
That the earth may have its rest,
For God so rules the seasons
To do what each knows best.

Soon winter will be coming,
And, when the time is right,
God will bed the weary traveler
With coverlet of white.

And, in that winter's sleeping,
What dreams live 'neath the snow?
One sunlit day next April
The grass will let us know.

Minnie Klemme

Photo Overleaf
AUTUMN FLOWERS
J. C. Benda

Photo Opposite
FROSTED LEAVES
WENATCHEE NATIONAL FOREST, WA
Ed Cooper Enterprises

Autumn Field

High overhead, the mellow sun at noon
Spills gold in payment for a locust's tune.
The faded-yellow cornstalk tents repose
In watchful attitudes, while circling crows

Spread raven wings against an azure sky
To startle field mice with their piercing cry.
Here, too, wild sumac crawls in scarlet stealth
Across brown vines once heavy with a wealth

Of plump blackberries, sweet beyond compare,
That tumbled in ripe confusion everywhere.
Now barren twigs emerge where summer's hand
Once laid a bright green pattern on the land,

And, though the earth is warm, my heart turns cold
With winds that warn me autumn's growing old.

Viney Wilder Endicott

Photo Overleaf
MAROON BELL MOUNTAIN, CC
Ed Cooper Enterprises

Photo Opposite
CHICKORY AND OATS
WASHINGTON ISLAND, WI
Gene Ahrens

October Song

It's showering yellow leaves today,
The lowmost limbs are bare,
And there's a lusty pungency,
Like challenge, in the air.

I'll take your challenge, Autumn,
Lay down my years, my load,
To roam like a child in the woodland
And down the river road.

Then when age makes me prisoner
This zest, this tang, shall stay
And set my old lips singing
It's showering leaves today!

Kunigunde Duncan

Photo Overleaf
MILL BROOK, VT
FPG International

Photo Opposite
ALBANY, NH
ed Sieb Photography

Fall Apples

The apples hang heavy on the branches now,
Bright scarlet, and mellowed by the sun's warm glow.
Fall's rich yield is everywhere
On the hill where the orchard sweetens the air.

I lose sight of the barn and the weathercock,
The stubbled fields where the summer grain was shocked.
For the trees with their heavy-laden limbs
Merge their branches and leaves and hedge me in.

I see with delight where apples lie on the ground,
Checkering the rich earth in scarlet and brown;
Where apples cling loosely to every stem,
And I have acres of trees to find the best gem!

At last, the apples I seek are ripe,
Sweet and crunchy and delightfully right;
Not like the one that once puckered my lips,
Green and stone-hard when I bit out a chip.

But off I must go to spread the word,
To the wren on the post, past the grazing herd,
To Father in the barn, lifting hay from the mow...
At last, the apples are ready to be gathered now!

Joy Belle Burgess

Photo Overleaf
CARPET OF COLOR
FPG International

Photo Opposite
APPLE ORCHARD
EGG HARBOR, WI
Ken Dequaine

Chrysanthemums

With summer and sun behind you,
    With winter and shade before,
You crowd in your regal splendor
    Through the autumn's closing door.
White as the snow that is coming,
    Red as the rose that is gone,
Gold as the heart of the lilies,
    Pink as the flush of the dawn.
Confident, winsome, stately,
    You throng in the wane of the year,
Trooping an army with banners
    When the leafless woods are sere.

Sweet is your breath as of spices
    From a far sea island blown;
Chaste your robes as of vestals
    Trimming their lamps alone.
Strong are your hearts, and sturdy
    The life that in root and stem

Smoulders and glows till it sparkles
    In each flowery diadem.
Nothing of bloom and odor
    Have your peerless legions lost,
Marching in fervid beauty
    To challenge the death-white frost.

So to the eye of sorrow
    You bring a flicker of light;
The cheek that was wan with illness
    Smiles at your faces bright.
The children laugh in greeting,
    And the dear old people say,
"Here are the selfsame darlings
    We loved in our own young day,"
As, summer and sun behind you,
    Winter and shade before,
You crowd in your regal splendor
    Through the autumn's closing door.

Margaret Elizabeth Sangster

Photo Opposite
CHRYSANTHEMUMS
FPG International

AUTUMN: *A Season of Contemplation*

ENCHANTED FOREST
Richard W. Brown

A *season of contemplation, a chance to remember days gone by and to plan new paths for the future.*

The Old Hometown

I want to go back to the old hometown,
   To a little white house all trimmed in brown;
To walk down the road where redbud sway,
   And sit 'neath the oaks where I used to play.

I want to see folks whom I used to know;
   I want to go places where I used to go.
I want to go down to the big dripping spring
   And sit on the moss where I used to sing.

I want to go back to the little church house,
   Where I used to go in my starched-up blouse,
Where the preacher would smile and kindly say:
   "My boy, I am glad you came today."

I want to go back to the old hometown,
   To a little white house all trimmed in brown,
To walk down the road where redbud sway
   And sit 'neath the oaks where I used to play.

                Cecil Brown

Photo Overleaf
COLCHESTER, CT
Fred M. Dole Productions

Photo Opposite
WESTON, VT
FPG International

The Road Not Taken

Two roads diverged in a yellow wood,
And sorry I could not travel both
And be one traveler, long I stood
And looked down one as far as I could
To where it bent in the undergrowth;

Then took the other, as just as fair,
And having perhaps the better claim,
Because it was grassy and wanted wear;
Though as for that, the passing there
Had worn them really about the same,

And both that morning equally lay
In leaves no step had trodden black.
Oh, I kept the first for another day!
Yet knowing how way leads on to way,
I doubted if I should ever come back.

I shall be telling this with a sigh
Somewhere ages and ages hence:
Two roads diverged in a wood, and I—
I took the one less traveled by,
And that has made all the difference.

Robert Frost

Photo Overleaf
ERKSHIRE HILLS, MA
Gene Ahrens

Photo Opposite
HOMECOMING
FPG International

September Comes in Quietly

September comes in quietly at Stillmeadow. The gardens in the valley are in full bloom. Sunlight sifts through the canopy of the giant maples—as it has all summer.

And yet I go out one morning and know that summer is drifting up the hill in the soft blue haze. And I feel an urgency to gather in all the loveliness of the past blazing days and star-cool nights and keep them forever. But fall is here. Goldenrod is splashing color along the road, and wild asters open their delicate amethyst petals. In the swamp, the first scarlet burns above the huckleberry bushes.

Days grow shorter now, and the first frost will come mid-month. Migrant birds leave according to their own mysterious schedule. Squirrels fling themselves from tree to tree in a burst of activity.

Now that so much of the woodlands has been destroyed, I sometimes wonder just how many dwellers there are in my woods and swamps. Most of the deer have gone, and this is a sad loss.

There are many things to do before the long cold sets in, but it is so easy to put them off. For this is a dreaming time and a time to be thankful. I do not want to miss the beauty of moonlight dipping into the pond, or the smell of wild grapes by the gray stone fence, or the sound of a katydid singing the requiem of summer.

Gladys Taber

Photo Overleaf
)UTH WOODBURY, VT
Bob Clemenz

Photo Opposite
HARVEST TIME
FPG International

All Times
Are His Seasons

We ask our daily bread, and God never says, You should have come yesterday. He never says, You must come again tomorrow. But "today if you will hear His voice," today He will hear you. If some king of the earth hath so large an extent of dominion in north and south as that he hath winter and summer together in his dominions, so large an extent of east and west as that he hath day and night together in his dominions, much more hath God mercy and judgment together. He brought light out of darkness, not out of a lesser light. He can bring thy summer out of winter though thou have no spring.

God made sun and moon to distinguish seasons, and day and night; and we cannot have the fruits of the earth but in their seasons. But God hath made no decrees to distinguish the seasons of His mercies. In Paradise the fruits were ripe the first minute, and in Heaven it is always autumn, His mercies are ever in their maturity.

John Donne

Photo Overleaf
NEW ENGLAND CHARM
Jack Zehrt

Photo Opposite
DRAMATIC DAYBREAK
H. Armstrong Roberts, Inc

November Woods

Lovely are the silent woods
 in gray November days,
When the leaves fall red and gold
 about the quiet ways,
From massive beech, majestic oak
 and birches white and slim,
Like the pillared aisles of a cathedral
 vast and dim.

Drifting mist like smoking incense
 hangs upon the air...
Along the paths where birds once sang
 the trees stand stripped and bare,
Making Gothic arches
 with their branches interlaced,
And windows framing vistas,
 richly wrought and finely traced.

It is good to be in such a place
 on such a day...
Problems vanish from the mind
 and sorrows steal away;
In the woods of gray November
 silent and austere,
Nature gives her benediction
 to the passing year.

Patience Strong

Photo Opposite
RAPIDS IN GATINEAU HILLS
LIMBOUR, QUEBEC, CANADA
Malak Photographs Ltd.

SAND HARBOR
LAKE TAHOE STATE PARK, NV
Ed Cooper Enterprises

A *season of rest, a chance for nature to
sleep in preparation for the coming spring.*

The Frost Spirit

He comes—he comes—the Frost Spirit comes! You may
    trace his steps now
On the naked woods and the blasted fields and the brown
    hill's withered brow.
He has smitten the leaves of the gray old trees where their
    pleasant green came forth,
And the winds, which follow wherever he goes, have shaken
    them down to earth.

He comes—he comes—the Frost Spirit comes! from the
    frozen Labrador,
From the icy bridge of the Northern seas, which the white
    bear wanders o'er,
Where the fisherman's sail is stiff with ice and the luckless
    forms below
In the sunless cold of the lingering night into marble statues
    grow!

He comes—he comes—the Frost Spirit comes! on the rush-
    ing Northern blast,
And the dark Norwegian pines have bowed as his fearful
    breath went past.
With an unscorched wing he has hurried on, where the fires of
    Helca glow
On the darkly beautiful sky above and the ancient ice below.

He comes—he comes—the Frost Spirit comes! Let us meet
    him as we may,
And turn with the light of the parlor-fire his evil power
    away;
And gather closer the circle round, when that firelight dances
    high,
And laugh at the shriek of the baffled Fiend as his sounding
    wing goes by!

John Greenleaf Whittier

Photo Overleaf
MORRISTOWN NATIONAL
HISTORICAL PARK, NJ
Gene Ahrens

Photo Opposite
FIRST FROST
YOSEMITE NATIONAL PARK, CA
Ed Cooper Enterprises

WICK HOUSE
MORRISTOWN, NEW JERSEY
Gene Ahrens

Winter in the Country

I think that country living finds its peak
In wintertime when fields are wrapped in snow,
When cellars bulge with little stored up things,
Barrels of salt pork, fruit standing row on row,
Bins of potatoes, apples in their prime.
For gracious living give me wintertime.

The summer's rush is over on the land,
Crops gathered in, sleek cattle in their stalls,
The sheep well-housed, the chickens contented,
While over all a sense of quiet falls
As if the earth were taking a short nap
Like an old woman in a woolen wrap.

The hills are white against the winter sky,
The meadows bedded down for winter sleep,
Old maple trees rock stiffly in the wind,
Around the farmhouse purple shadows creep,
A lighted window sends a shaft of light
Into the darkness of the winter night.

How good a life can be that holds unto
The sane and simple ways of Mother Earth,
Whole days are lived with piety and grace
Acquainted with the ways of death and birth,
Yet holding ever in his calloused hand
The quiet strength and beauty of the land.

Edna Jaques

Photo Overleaf
CATSKILL MOUNTAINS, N
H. Armstrong Roberts, Inc

Photo Opposite
SNOW COVERED BRIDG
NEW ENGLAND
FPG International

Ice

A world encased in
ice, a glittering
crystal world,
extends around me.
During the night,
fine, freezing rain
drifted down, and on
this mid-January
morning the rising
sun highlights
gray birches burdened
with ice and
bending low,
snowdrifts armor-
plated with glaring
crusts, stone walls
sheathed in smooth,
transparent shells.

Edwin Way Teale

Photo Overleaf
WINTER'S SPARKLE
WESTERN CT
dex Stock International, Inc.

Photo Opposite
EVERGREEN BOUGH
NORTH CONWAY, NH
Fred Sieb Photography

Mountain Pines

The snows fall deep, the snows fall fast,
And the lights are out of the sky;
The moan, oh, the moan of the winter wind,
And its wail as it scurries by!

The laurel-brake and the maidenhair
Seem dead as the hopes of May;
I stand alone beneath the pines,
And the mountains stretch away.

The wolf's hoarse howl, the jackal's bay,
Or the least of nature's signs
Would music, welcome music be
Amid these mountain pines.

From the cold gray earth to the cold gray sky
They reach like plummet lines,
And I am but an unseen speck
Amid these mountain pines.

W.T.W. Barbe

Photo Overleaf
GRANDVIEW POINT
GRAND CANYON NATIONAL PARK, AZ
Ed Cooper Enterprises

Photo Opposite
EL CAPITAN
YOSEMITE NATIONAL PARK, CA
Ken Carlson

Holly Fairies

Oh, fairies love a holly tree—
The foliage makes a roof
of sturdy shingles,
always green
and new and weatherproof.

And even under winter skies
the berries burn so bright
they look like
little fairy lamps
with bulbs of crimson light.

Oh, fairies love a holly spray
too much by far to leave,
and so they up and follow it
indoors on Christmas Eve.

And that is why each house
is blessed
where holly sprigs are seen,
because the fairies
still are there
beneath the red and green.

Aileen Fisher

Photo Opposite
HOLLY
NEW BRUNSWICK, NJ
FPG International

THE MERCED RIVER
YOSEMITE NATIONAL PARK, C
Ed Cooper Enterprises

A *season of reflection, a relaxing time to reminisce about the year soon to end while slowly moving into the months ahead.*

The Brook

The tireless brook through winter's snows
Pursues its course and onward goes
O'er twig and stone, now left, now right,
It winds its way by day and night
As if in haste to find the chance
To join the ocean's vast expanse.

The trees that grace its ragged bank
Like sentinels on either flank
Stand staunch and steadfast through the years,
Dispelling winter's snow-bound fears,
And giving forth the promise true
That soon the summer will be due.

The house that dots the distant hill
Now feels the winter's icy chill,
But soon the warming sun will come
And cause the snow to swiftly run
To join the rushing brook in glee
That now its action will be free.

How like the brook we humans are,
We ever seek that goal afar
Where we shall merge our lives at last
In seas whose depths engulf the past,
Whose shores bid us our struggles cease
And live henceforth in perfect peace.

George Z. Keller

Photo Overleaf
GRAFTON, VT
pel Color Photography

Photo Opposite
DELIGHTED DUCKS
FPG International

Beautiful, Beautiful Snow

A winter world's a soft white world
  Of drifts and glistening flakes
And boughs and overhangings high
  And sculptured pristine lakes.
And often in this magnitude
  Of soft white driven snow
Are footprints small, belonging to
  Some creature on the go,
  Who stood and smelled the clear crisp air
  Then tracked upon his way...
  Excited by the wonderworld
  That held the land in sway.

O winter world, O soft white world,
  In you I see God's touch,
And feel that He created you
  For those He loves so much.

  A promise too is there ahead,
  For when the snow has gone
  He'll leave His springtime world for us
  To love and look upon!

Nelle Hardgrove

Photo Overleaf
WEST NEWBURY, VT
Fred M. Dole Productions

Photo Opposite
CAVENDISH, VT
Robert Holland

Belief

I do not always understand
The many things I see:
The hills that climb to meet the sky,
The shore that finds the sea,
A shining star at close of day
As twilight gathers near,
And then the darkness all about
As night is quickly here.

I do not always analyze
The things before my eyes:
The mysteries too deep to know,
The hours of sweet surprise,
A stream that flows through valleys deep,
The river rushing on,
The desert sand so dry and still,
The day that's here and gone.

Belief is mine; although 'tis true
I know not how or why,
The rain shall end as it began
And sunshine light the sky.
'Tis faith alone that tells my heart
The winter too shall pass,
And spring will come to bless the world
An April day at last.

I cannot always understand
These miracles of God;
But one day all of us shall walk
The path that angels trod.
Still, I believe and always shall
In so much yet unseen;
Because a faith lives in my heart,
Belief is mine supreme.

Garnett Ann Schultz

Photo Overleaf
WEST NEWBURY, VT
Fred M. Dole Productions

Photo Opposite
A WINTERY MORN
The Photo Source

Bare Boughs

The bare boughs reach across the windowpane.
It's hard to think they'll ever live again.
It seems to me a thing incredible
That there could be so great a miracle.

So dead they look seen from this firelit room,
Dark and stark against the wintry gloom.
And yet this day unto that gnarled old tree
There came a blackbird with a prophecy.

Out of the grayness of the sky he flew
Into the branches where the cold winds blew,
And boldly he prophesied this wondrous thing,
Filling the garden with a dream of spring.

Patience Strong

Photo Opposite
LYMPIC STATE PARK, WA
Ed Cooper Enterprises

View of the Valley

Pursuing my lonely way down the valley, I turned again and again to gaze on the glorious picture, throwing up my arms to enclose it as in a frame. After long ages of growth in the darkness beneath the glaciers, through sunshine and storms, it seemed now to be ready and waiting for the elected artist, like yellow wheat for the reaper; and I could not help wishing that I might carry colors and brushes with me on my travels, and learn to paint. In the meantime I had to be content with photographs on my mind and sketches in my notebooks. At length, after I had rounded a precipitous headland that puts out from the west wall of the valley, every peak vanished from sight, and I pushed rapidly along the frozen meadows, over the divide between the waters of the Merced and Tuolumne, and down through the forests that clothe the slopes of Cloud's Rest, arriving in Yosemite in due time — which, with me, is *any* time.

John Muir

Photo Overleaf
JONQUIL
Ina Mackey

EL CAPITAN
YOSEMITE NATIONAL PARK, CA
Pedley/Tom Stack & Associates